The "After" Life

Steven Bates

STEVEN BATES

Also available from Steven Bates

Reflections of a Beret

Forgotten Places

Caleuche Chronicles

The "After" Life

STEVEN BATES

Acknowledgements

The reason for titling this book "The 'After' Life" is simple; this book and the poems within, with one or two exceptions, were written after my military service and during my road to healing. Hence the picture on the cover, a military tradition signifying that you are leaving a base behind you. I have so many people to thank for believing in me and encouraging my writing which has resulted in not just one book, but now a second one. I didn't write my poems for monetary gain or fame. I write to let others know there are many out there with the same feelings regarding life in general, struggles with depression, PTSD, suicide and post-military attitudes. This book is for everyone and those who care for them.

Many people have influenced my writing in one way or another. Some have indirectly affected me in the different avenues of life, while others have directly influenced me. Other events such as race riots, political discourse, election debates, class warfare, and others have driven me to write poems of the world without having a specific individual in mind. These events affect the world and need a calm response. My poetry is my only path to peacefully comment.

The influences that directly affect my life are more precious: my amazing, incredible wife, Sandra, without whom I know I would be back into an institutionalized state. She has been my rock, my comfort, and my inspiration in every situation. My parents; my children (every one of them, whether they believe it or not), and my dear friends: I couldn't have made it thru this thing called Life without them.

My thanks go to my publisher, Josh Walker, from Forgotten Places Publishing and my dear friend Maeke. Josh believed in my poems helping others enough to publish both of my books and Maeke believed in me from the time she heard me recite a poem competing for the National Veterans' Creative Arts Festival. Thanks to the few and precious in my life, and thanks to the masses which had no clue they were giving me inspiration. I couldn't have done this without each and every one of you. Thank you!

STEVEN BATES

Dedication

To my Father, who inspired my dreams

of following in his footsteps,

To my Mother, who gave me my dreams of hope,

To my Wife, who fulfilled my dreams.

STEVEN BATES

Contents

Patriotism

Old Glory

Old Glory flaps loudly, so high in the breeze
As my hand raises quickly with a well-practiced ease
In respect, Present Arms, for the cloth of our land
As below at attention I humbly do stand

I think of the men that carried Her forth into battle
On their shoulders, they bore Her while sabers did rattle
As gunfire and rockets pressed on the attack
Our men never faltered, they never turned back

They knew that the symbol of our nation so great
Is also a target for those filled with hate
Yet they carried Her high with pride and conviction
In all of our battles, our wars, interdictions

She flew with the greatest and lowliest of those
Who fought for our freedoms, and evil opposed
From the youngest of privates to the eldest with stars
She's known by her colors, the red and white bars

Her blue filled with stars, each a state by their right
As United they stand, and United they fight
So the next time you see Her, atop a tall pole
Remember She flies for your nation, its' soul

She's lowered in reverence as the day's work is through
And folded with honor, as my hand comes down too

Thoughts and Reflections

_____

_____

_____

_____

_____

_____

_____

_____

_____

_____

_____

_____

_____

_____

STEVEN BATES

Advice to the Civilian

So you're thinking of joining
Of giving your all
And you're tired of hanging
Around at the mall

Feeling like serving
This Nation so great
The desire is burning
To be proud of your state

You'll lift up your hand
Take a solemn, revered oath
To protect this great land
Here and over there both

You'll wake before dawn
For PT in the morn
And you'll do something wrong
To earn your Instructor's scorn

You'll march every day
Till the boots are worn thin
But you'll be earning pay
That amounts to a sin

Low wages you'll get
And overworked hard
But you'll be lean and fit
And this Nation you'll guard

You'll serve in such places
You've never heard of before
And see things and faces
Too much to keep score

One thing I can tell you
About your time serving now
Is to be brave and true
And honor your vow

Honor, Duty, Commitment and Courage
You'll soon feel these all
From your Boot Camp tutelage
And stand proud and tall

To a school, you'll head out
To learn craft and trade
And graduating shout
That a career you have made

For you now stand one of us
With no glory or fame
No muss and no fuss
A Veteran now is your name

14

Thoughts and Reflections

_____

_____

_____

_____

_____

_____

_____

_____

_____

_____

_____

_____

_____

_____

_____

_____

Where Has Our Patriotism Gone?

It swelled in the hearts of the brave warriors who died
And beat ever strong in those blessed to survive
It echoed 'round tombstones and crypts of those passed
On porches and front yards when parades ambled past

It coursed through veins of those taking the oath
To protect against forces that Americans loathe
The evils of dictators, tyrants, and kings,
The hardships of subjects trapped under such things

It was found in the foxholes, in bunkers and tanks
In the heartbeats of soldiers, no matter the ranks
It was felt in the pledge to our flag and our land
Held true in the hearts of those who fought in the sand,

In the jungles, the rice fields, the Bavarian hills,
Wherever we're fighting, wherever blood spills
It was found in the fathers, the mothers, and wives
The husbands and brothers, those who gave their lives

It was once displayed everywhere for the whole world to see
With flags waving on houses in the Land of the Free
But now it's sadly sequestered for fear of offending
Those here with intentions of freedom upending
We've forgotten our pledge, for our anthem, some kneel
I ask you America, please, WHAT'S THE DEAL?

Thoughts and Reflections

_____

_____

_____

_____

_____

_____

_____

_____

_____

_____

_____

_____

_____

_____

Freedom

It's not a where: a set location
It's not a what: a country or nation
It's not a who: a person or man
It's not a when: a time or plan
It's not a why, though it came from oppression
It's not a reason, but an answer to a question
It's not an idea, though it's forged from the fires
Of tyranny, and conquest, of all man desires

It is simply the rights that every man dreams
As he struggles to push through society's schemes
The rights that are dreamed of are a real simple fare
Life first, then liberty, an indomitable pair
Pursuit of Happiness is the last of the three
But it's no more the lesser, and not meant to be

The right to pursue doesn't mean guaranteed
But that we have the power to plant just a very small seed
That up from this kernel of truth, hope and grace
We'll all co-exist, regardless of race
With Freedom to guide us, and freedom to grow
I pray thee Almighty, let all this be so.

The "After" Life

Thoughts and Reflections

_____

_____

_____

_____

_____

_____

_____

_____

_____

_____

_____

_____

_____

_____

_____

_____

Changes

Life hands us lessons as we grow
For some a little too late
For all the things that we should know
To make our lives and nation great

We tend to learn from our mistakes
Instead of learning ahead
And all the changes that we make
Are from reacting instead

Why must we learn in this horrible way
When given such troubling news
And what do we do, and what do we say
when this changes all of our views?

For the knowledge we so deeply yearn
To prevent so much of this pain
Are simply methods we all must learn
For peace our souls to gain

We seem to know before the facts
If our actions will harm others
Yet still we keep committing acts
That hurt our kindred brothers

It's time my friends to gather round
And help instead of hinder
All to whom can hear this sound
Of kindness soft and tender

Reach out to those and heed the calls
Of duty, honor, glory
And act before this nation falls
That's it, the end of story

Thoughts and Reflections

_____

_____

_____

_____

_____

_____

_____

_____

_____

_____

_____

_____

_____

_____

_____

STEVEN BATES

Blue Souls

5 souls at least died on that night
As black on blue engaged in fight
A sniper ambushed police they say
With seven more wounded to add to the fray

Then another one wounded, another cop died
Another night of terror in our hearts reside
The President announced that guns were the reason
That our men in blue have been declared open season

That souls behind badges were the most feared of all
As many more died answering their nation's call
Or they passed away when ambushed from
The cowardly, villainous, heartless scum

How many must die from this much-misplaced anger
That threatens cop's lives with even more danger?
For how many dead does it take to appease?
And how many graves must we dig then to please?

How many shall die for the acts of a few?
How long until citizens start backing the Blue?
How many souls must as sacrifice die?
With the actions of thugs as heroes belie

For it's not heroism when a cop you attack
Whose deep fear of racism prevents fighting back
And these souls have their children, their families, and spouse
When upon the Blue dying, lose their income, their house

Their passion for living is just taken away
By some radical thug trying to make the cops pay
But no actions were taken by those innocents lost
Though killed they were in this gross holocaust

They did nothing wrong, except wearing the Blue
And living to serve and protect even you
Yes, Blue souls are dying from hate every day
And it's time to Back Blue, and make criminals pay

Instead of parading the families of thugs
Let us Back the Blue, give them prayers, give them hugs
Let them all know that you're on their side
And with hope, and support, no more Blue Souls will die.

Thoughts and Reflections

_____

_____

_____

_____

_____

_____

_____

_____

_____

_____

_____

_____

_____

_____

Race

Race haters, race baiters, all are the same
A life is taken and we all rush to blame
We disregard facts, based on skewed bits from some phone
When we probably would have done the same on our own

Tensions are high now, in fact off the scale
By people clamoring to convict, and even to kill
They'd rather attack and create a race war
Where innocent lives lost, fuel the fire even more

By ignoring all facts, basing convictions on race
We all have become what we fought hard to erase
We won the Great War where all men were freed
But it doesn't seem to matter when we planted that seed

The last hundred years we spent repairing the rifts
Between races, sexes, and all freedoms' gifts
We find fault with others based on skin color alone
And march in with violence until someone is prone

It matters not of whom the blue blood spills red
As long as there's justice for somebody dead
Can't you see America, that's no way to end
No way to stop that horrific trend

But if just one American stands ready for peace
Instead of the bloodshed all over the streets
Stand up for America, don't surrender and fall
I implore, nay I beg, for this madness to halt

And stop putting skin color above all the throng
This us versus them mentality's wrong!

The "After" Life

Thoughts and Reflections

_____

_____

_____

_____

_____

_____

_____

_____

_____

_____

_____

_____

_____

_____

_____

STEVEN BATES

War and Peace

It's Quiet Enough

The sounds were agonizing to my ears
Fulfilling all my nightmarish fears
And when the going got tough I went into the fray
But it's quiet enough here now where I lay

When screams and bullets passed me by
But it's quiet enough here where I lie
And land mines met those who bravely went
To charge ahead as leather hell bent

And the noises have faded, why I can't say
But it's quiet enough here where I lay
I can't see the foe or fires from here
And the silence is deafening to my ear

The world is black to my shut eyes
Still, it's quiet enough, here where I lie
I've found the peace in war and hell
Where once was noise, it's clear as a bell

Where once were anguish and my worst fears
The calm now has allayed my tears
When I charged ahead I feared to die
But it's quiet enough here where I lie

Thoughts and Reflections

_____

_____

_____

_____

_____

_____

_____

_____

_____

_____

_____

_____

_____

_____

_____

The Cemetery

Standing before a sobering sight
Of alabaster headstones polished white
Inlaid crosses, stars of David
The older names are all but faded

Dates of birth with dates of death
Defending peace with their last breath
Flags adorn the marble stones
To honor named and those unknowns

They earned their rest, they earned respect
So we honor them and genuflect
We plant the flags, we have parades
In order to give them accolades
We salute and tip our drinks to those
Who gave their lives in fighting foes

We place a coin on markers there
To show we knew them, to show we care
To show the world we knew them well
And honor those who in combat fell

We honor those who for our country died
Defending Freedom, there's no greater pride
And so in reverence, I walk among these stones
For those who paid the cost, let them be known
To respect them all that paid the price
and gave the ultimate in sacrifice

Thoughts and Reflections

_____

_____

_____

_____

_____

_____

_____

_____

_____

_____

_____

_____

_____

_____

Peace

Whistling balls of heated lead
Zinging past my sheltered head
Whooshing missiles launched nearby
Seeking Scuds to safe the sky

Booms from aircraft dropping loads
And firing cannons to secure the roads
Sounds of battles, screams of pain
As shrapnel fell like fiery rain

I can't recall the pain I felt
If I fell or if I knelt
Did I give a decent fight,
Or did I merely lose my light?

For here I lay, the sounds are gone
Above me stretches a manicured lawn
The peace and quiet I thought I'd crave
Pounds on my ears while in my grave

But softly above a nation mourns
A flag is folded, a wreath adorns
My stone reads simply "Here he lies"
"No more battle in his eyes"

"No more screams for him to hear"
Then marked by name, a date, a year
I lie here, resting in peace, they say
Some crowds would come, and some would pray

But though rest is free from war's loud din
I'd give all this peace to fight again
So truly think of those beneath
As you plant flags, or place a wreath

For they kept you safe and our nation free
As was their oath, their humble decree
Memorial Day honors those who fell
As we play Taps, or ring a bell
Though in peace they lay beneath a stone
Their silence echoes, their great deeds unknown

Thoughts and Reflections

_____

_____

_____

_____

_____

_____

_____

_____

_____

_____

_____

_____

_____

_____

_____

Holiday Hopes

Christmas comes and Christmas goes
Meanwhile, still I fight my foes
The New Year brings a festive night
As I track a target in my sights

Cupid's arrow hits the mark
While I listen for our K-9's bark
Easter Sunday brings all to Mass
While I dodge debris from bomber's blast

Then Mother's Day, Memorial Day
Pass on by while I earn my pay
Now the patriot pride of the 4th of July
As missiles and rockets light my sky

Labor Day, Veteran's Day, Thanksgiving too
Just three more days that I miss you
Christmas comes and on patrol I roam
Just one more year that I'm not home

Yet worry not loved ones that I'm not there
For dying alone is my greatest fear
So have faith my loved ones, and be of good cheer
I'll make it home safely, by the end of this year

Thoughts and Reflections

_____

_____

_____

_____

_____

_____

_____

_____

_____

_____

_____

_____

_____

_____

STEVEN BATES

Stinger Duty

Alone with my partner on top of a hill
Manning our Stingers for the "One shot, one kill"
Positioned tactically around the whole base
With camouflaged vehicle, camouflaged face

Our eyes ever alert and watching the skies
Repeating our mantra, "If it flies, it dies"
The radio crackles with a bogey inbound
With bearing and speed, our hearts start to pound

We look to the heavens as our sweat starts to bead
A speck in the distance is all that we need
My partner then spots it with eyes like a hawk
I aim with my Stinger, a tone confirms lock

And the heartbeat that follows is pure agony
'Til the IFF, (Friend or Foe), notifies me
The plane in question, that tiny little spot
Is a friendly inbound, and a target it's not

The radio confirms then the bogey's no threat
So we unlock the Stinger, breathe a sigh, wipe the sweat
So close was this pilot to a death by mistake
For a Stinger won't miss, not for anyone's sake
Ninety plus nine is the percent it will hit
It's the best duty I've had, bar none, and that's it.

Thoughts and Reflections

_____

_____

_____

_____

_____

_____

_____

_____

_____

_____

_____

_____

_____

_____

Desensitized

He called out bingo numbers in the dry desert heat
Boredom for the troops he was trying to beat
Till the thunderous boom in the distance they heard
Which meant 'head to the shelter', a mortar they feared

As each of them scrambled for a place in the bunker
Most donned their gear and in shelter did hunker
While most prayed for grace, there were a few of the men
Who whined that there wouldn't be Bingo to win

They fussed and they fumed, not a thought to their plight
They thought more of their game than the overall fight
It saddened him greatly as no care was given
To the chance they may not soon be among the living

The explosions around him were making him think
How fast he could die here, before his next blink
He thought of his family, his friends and his wife
How he might not be able to be a part of their lives

Then he looked back at the troops still whining away

All on their minds was the game they can't play

They've been desensitized by their Wii's and Playstations

With generated explosions and graphics of wars of all nations

Never once did they realize the danger they were in

Or that two Airmen in blue would call next of kin

Never a moment did they panic or think of their wives

For these bombings had become such a part of their lives

The 'all clear' alarms then screeched to return

Back to duties and Bingo; the life that they yearned

Desensitized they were and how he wished he could be

But all he could think of was across the sea

It was more than enough to convince him it's time

To put in his papers and live life sublime

Once he returned, he'd retire in style

All that was needed was the form he could file

His thoughts then returned to the young troops complaining

And how many of them would at the end be remaining

They felt no compassions for the plight that they're in

Desensitized by their games, they just wanted to win

He mulled their bravado, their courage under fire

How the situations were deadly, the conditions so dire

His thoughts so intense the boom wasn't heard

As the mortar that landed ended their world

Thoughts and Reflections

_____

_____

_____

_____

_____

_____

_____

_____

_____

_____

_____

_____

_____

_____

_____

After

After the heartaches, after the pains
After the leeches from life have you drained
After the storms, and after the rains
After the lessons of life have you trained

After a lifetime of doubt leaves you jaded
After a shattering of dreams that you made
After all hope of surviving has faded
After the foundation of lies have been laid

After your hand of cards have been played
After the backstabbing and being betrayed
After the assassin has inserted the blade
After your losses have gotten you frayed

After you're ready to begin all anew
After you've decided your old life is through
After that moment, after facing that fact
Then by all means change, start now and react!

Thoughts and Reflections

_____

_____

_____

_____

_____

_____

_____

_____

_____

_____

_____

_____

_____

_____

_____

STEVEN BATES

Forgotten Feelings

So lost in time and lost in thought
Are memories before the wars were fought
A time of peace and pleasant dreams
Before the time of nightmarish screams

A time when joy was brought on by smells
And not ruined by death's own tolled bells
When laughter filled the parks with glee
Not with moans of agony

When sight beheld their loved one's hair
Instead, crosshairs come to bear
A time when smiles meant merriment
Not sardonic grins of the terror-bent

When lightened touch from skin or breath
Was not a cold and clammy brush with Death
Fear not, those loved ones left behind
You're still there in back of mind

You're not forgotten, you are why we're here
To prevent those wars from coming near
You're not forgotten, You're why we live
From day to day our all we give

You're not forgotten, we'll come home to you
To ensure those memories all ring true

Thoughts and Reflections

_____

_____

_____

_____

_____

_____

_____

_____

_____

_____

_____

_____

_____

_____

STEVEN BATES

Affairs of the Heart

Lest I...

Lest I Die before my time,
Lest my breath becomes my last
Lest the church bells for me chime
Lest my time on Earth is past

Lest my final kiss goodbye
Is given with the kiss of life
Lest the flag flies halfway high
And folded given to my wife

Lest the rifles break the silence
As Taps is played in mournful tones
Lest my life's forgotten hence
With naught to show but skin and bones

Lest I pass I must make amends
To all my family, near and distant
To all my enemies, all my friends
I must be fair, must be consistent

For lest I Die before my time
May Heaven's gate allow me in
And may I cherish sweet peace sublime
When He alone absolved my sin

But lest I fail repent my ways
And finish life with sin intact
Then Hell would welcome me to stay
Lest Heaven fights to take me back

Lest my life ends without His grace
And my soul burns eternally
Then to all my children you must face
This poem is my ministry

Thoughts and Reflections

Last Words

My dying words were uttered

But were not said in vain

For the one that heard them uttered

Was He that exiled Cain

My comfort, the immortal one

Who died to set me free

The Father, Spirit, and the Son

He cared that much for me

He took my sins and let me live

On Earth so peacefully

And though I'm dead, I have to give

In Heaven, my love,

Eternally

Thoughts and Reflections

_____

_____

_____

_____

_____

_____

_____

_____

_____

_____

_____

_____

_____

_____

Forgotten Feelings II

So lost in time and lost in thought
Are memories before the wars were fought
A time of peace and pleasant dreams
A moment before nightmarish screams

A sliver of solace, a minute of quiet
Before all the mobs had begun to riot
When all brother man would be there as a friend
And would back up your life to the very end

A heartbeat really in the vastness of time
When mankind existed at their very prime
For once we survived with each other in mind
When humanity once worried about dealing in kind

We cared for our brethren, our sisters, our kin
Now why can't we go back to that time again?
It was only a flash in the span of our lives
But loving and kindness were humanities' drives

Not greed, not hate, nor revenge or wealth
But our questing for answers to life and good health
We held on to peace, we talked problems out
Forgiveness was key to what life was about

If only those feelings, forgotten in time
We could once again have, with peace so sublime
So I challenge you brothers and sisters in life
Step away from the anger, the hatred, the strife

Learn once again those feelings of old
And step into the warmth, out of the cold
Celebrate the life, the air that you breathe
And Peace unto you, and may Joy you bequeath

Thoughts and Reflections

Voices on My Shoulder

Nagging voices, whining pleas
To do the worst of evil deeds
Taunting to my ear so close
I feel his breath, so cold, morose

I feel his eyes on every move
He bids me follow, for him behoove
He tasks me to commit such crimes
As befitting evil in these times

His words spoke softly so not to scare
This evil from me, next to my ear
He speaks of fortune, fame, and glory
If only I would hear his story

And right the wrongs he claims are true
From leaving Heaven before his due
He needs my arms, my hands, my feet
To spread his evil thru the street

He thinks he has my will convinced
That evil must right now commence
But one small flaw he fails to see
Is that there's another voice on me

From the right just at my shoulder
Rings a voice crisp, clear and bolder
It calmly states that I am His
And He'll protect my soul from Satan's kiss

So as I brush my shoulder, with calm I say
Lead me Dear Lord, for you're here to stay

Thoughts and Reflections

_____

_____

_____

_____

_____

_____

_____

_____

_____

_____

_____

_____

_____

_____

_____

STEVEN BATES

The Blade

Lightning fast, the Blade struck true,
Past the flesh, past the sinew
From its path, the Blade, never did it part
Until it struck, deep in my heart

It burned away a wound so deep
That crippled the heart though no blood did seep
It caused a hole, a great cavity
Too painful to watch, too horrific to see

It cut all ties that bound love to me
Like Family, and Bloodlines, both severed free
The Blade then twisted, pulling slowly out
Never knowing the hurt so flung about

My eyes glanced down, as love dripped away
From the damaged heart, the Blade did fillet
This Blade, a dagger, thrust in from the rear
From those I held close, that I still love dear

For only the pain of a loved one's stab
Can hurt so deep with no blood, no scab
So from my hollowed out heart I beg then plea
Don't let your love die in your family

Fight to keep it, work to get along
And never give up, keep Family love strong

The "After" Life

Thoughts and Reflections

_____

_____

_____

_____

_____

_____

_____

_____

_____

_____

_____

_____

_____

_____

_____

_____

Prayer

On bended knee I plead for aid
For help in all my worries
And at His feet my burdens laid
For to answer all my queries

My hopes, my dreams, my shattered plans
His answers may upset me
But all is made in His loving hands
In my strife, he shows such mercy

For He alone can quell my fears
And calm my trembling heart
To show me that my prayers He hears
And from my side, He'll never part

I rise with tears dried upon my face
As His hand my heart it yearns
I meet the day, renewed with grace
As He comforts all concerns

He guides my feet, for He's cleared a way
And on my shoulder rests His hand
To gently nudge, to softly sway
As I walk upon this land

In His embrace I step with God
My Savior in all His glory
He leads me, as thru life I trod
To live His life, His story

Thoughts and Reflections

_____

_____

_____

_____

_____

_____

_____

_____

_____

_____

_____

_____

_____

_____

_____

STEVEN BATES

Nature-ly

Butterflies

Patterns of black and patterns of blue

On flimsy wings of a lovely hue

Gracefully kissing the wind beneath

To find what flowers to them bequeath

Pollen dust and nectar cling

As the delicate butterfly takes wing

The flowers this gentle touch has blessed

Bloom brighter, stronger, than all the rest

And as the diaphanous wings flap ever slight

The intricate dance with flowers takes flight

Thoughts and Reflections

_____

_____

_____

_____

_____

_____

_____

_____

_____

_____

_____

_____

_____

_____

_____

STEVEN BATES

Dusk

Reds that scream a burning desire

Golds that burst as if on fire

Colors muted on the earth below

As if somehow the mountains know

To honor the sky, the sun and clouds

As they grow dim and dark enshrouds

The green of trees, of bushes of plants

'Til morning arises for the next day's dance

Thoughts and Reflections

_____

_____

_____

_____

_____

_____

_____

_____

_____

_____

_____

_____

_____

_____

_____

_____

STEVEN BATES

Through the Eyes of Trees

Silent witness to the world beneath
Of wars, of peace, of joy and grief
Standing tall, stretching above
The hate filled hearts, those filled with love

Looking down with saddened eyes
As humanity struggles hard and tries
to achieve the regal majesty
of a such a simple towering tree

The leaves part softly as eyes behold
Men moving as ants, if truth be told
For above the roots, below the branches
The Men perform their foolish dances

Like scattering roaches when light reveals
Their futile efforts, spinning their heels
They cannot grasp the wonders here
Of each tree's rings, time marked by years

Each recording in simple ways
The ebb of life, the flow of days
'Til the day that man looks up and sees
How they appear through the eyes of trees

Thoughts and Reflections

Forgotten Forest

Whispers whisk through weeping willows
Clouds hang down as puffy pillows
Fireflies flicker like fallen stars
Mist-eyed moths the moonlight mars

While crickets chirp in cadence clear
The forest beckons man to fear
None dare go near the towering trees
Which place many a man on bended knee

Outside the wondrous wooded glade
"Protection please" the pious prayed
For hopes that courage keep them strong
In places man dares try to belong

In this tree-bound temple tendrils trail
From swaying saplings, switches swell
As raindrops roll round reeded ponds,
Flowers bloom from bloated fronds

When padded paws press partial paths
And slithering scales slink sideways swathes
Red rimmed eyes like lasered lens
Peer to ponder foe or friends

Who swallows fear, sets pride aside
And dares to wander deep inside
Rewarding faith with findings fair
As forgotten forests are treasures rare
Affairs of the Heart

Thoughts and Reflections

_____

_____

_____

_____

_____

_____

_____

_____

_____

_____

_____

_____

_____

_____

_____

_____

Timeless

Babies fingers wrapped tight around
Babies crying, their very first sound
Infants crawling then learning to walk
Toddlers expressing their nature to balk

Little ones laughing while you and they play
Children off to school on their very first day
Teenagers learning to drive while you frown
Teenagers graduating, with cap and a gown

Now in their 20's with a thesis to write
Coming home from college, oh what a sight
These are just a few moments in the great span of a time
All timeless memories, all moments sublime

Timeless and wondrous, these brief snapshots of life
Oft taken for granted and forgotten with strife
But cherished so much in the dusk of your years
As twilight approaches and eyes swell with tears

Your child, your children, are what you're here for
And those timeless moments a gift ever more
So treasure those moments, your glimpses of joy
And thank your Creator for every girl, every boy

For all those seconds will add life to your smile
And a smile is so timeless, making it all worthwhile.

Thoughts and Reflections

STEVEN BATES

The Clergy's Voice

Gathered before us in reverence today
Are two that true love has held in sway
To marry each other for better or worse
To hold with each other, and in life, immerse

That always, as one, they are from this now
As they hold hands and make firm this most sacred of vow
Two hearts merge as one, and beating so fast
In hopes their true love and pure joy will long last

A lifetime together from this date they will plan
And give support to each other as best as they can
Lifting the other in times of great pain
And in sickness care for them, 'til health they regain

For richer or poorer they agree to remain
Forsaking all others, from adultery refrain
As I look down on their faces one question I ask
If any oppose them, then take them to task

Speak up at this moment if doubts you may bear
For this one final chance your concerns we can hear
If no one protests then this union of souls
Slide the rings on each finger, and "I dos" are then told

It's time I present then this couple to all
As a kiss seals the deal, and one they are called
What's been done here today let no person destroy
And may they live life forever, in peace, love, and joy

The "After" Life

Thoughts and Reflections

The Target

Staring through the iron sight
Barrel held so trembling tight
Target moves as to prove its life
Causing tension sharp as a knife

Finger gradually turning white
As it grips the trigger ever slight
Simple squeeze as breath is held
Recoil on cheek was all that's felt

With no reaction, no ego thrill
Shot was taken, hope for a kill
Looking forward with pensive frown
Target vanished, but was it down?

A moment later the target lifts
And moves its frame in ever swift
Steel and pulleys move with ease
As the paper target flaps with the breeze
My son, he lifts the rifle from where he lay
As I pray paper targets is all he'll have to slay

Thoughts and Reflections

STEVEN BATES

I Never Grieved

I never grieved,
Tears never fell
Even though when you passed
It put me through Hell

You once said I was strong
For not shedding my tears,
Now was I so wrong
After all of these years?

For life got in the way
Of my time and my grief
Though I now kneel and I pray
For just some relief

I held it all in,
Rather stoically so
For why should tears win
When you'll never know

Of how much I cared
And the pain that I felt
The one time I dared
And the blow that was dealt

I just couldn't handle
To tell you good-bye
And snuff out the candle
To let our love die

Yes, I never grieved
But my sorrow will hold
Till I stand relieved
On the streets of pure gold

Thoughts and Reflections

STEVEN BATES

Till The End

The warmth of her sleep still fresh on her skin
As I lean slowly down, and kiss her forehead again
She stirs ever slightly, but her dreams don't diminish
The clock screams an alarm for her sleep to now finish

Her eyes open slowly as if to dare the sun shine
She then hits the snooze for a few moments' time
Her nose, so adorable, then picks up the scent
Of the coffee beside her; for her, it's Heaven sent

She grabs hold of my arm to pull herself up
Reaching out quickly for that jolt in a cup
Her eyes more in focus as she mumbles her greetings
We speak our "I love yous" 'til the moment is fleeting

She rises from bed as a whiff of her hair
Flutters between us and smells oh so fair
As fair as her skin, and as light as her touch
She brushes beside me, God, I love her so much

She looks back and smiles a demurely sly grin
As I look in her eyes I thank Heaven again
For the gift in my life I call my dear friend
My partner and wife, I am hers 'til the end

The "After" Life

Thoughts and Reflections

_____

_____

_____

_____

_____

_____

_____

_____

_____

_____

_____

_____

_____

_____

_____

_____

_____

STEVEN BATES

Heartbreak

Tread lightly on my broken heart
Step soft on shattered valves
Fractured were they when told to part
And divide our lives in halves

For it held your love so tight within
And broke when so betrayed
Burst into shards from all your sin
Its flame no longer stayed

The pieces fell from such a height
From the pedestal where I placed you
Their falling with extinguished light
As pain refreshed anew

Shattered suffering, tormented tears
Release me from this anguish
As we throw away the many years
And my heart strings you relinquish

The "After" Life

Thoughts and Reflections

81

The "After" Life

Thoughts and Reflections

81

Betrayed

Behind the back barbed insults fly

While facing, smiles, intents belie

The blade parts flesh, inserted deep

And laughter echoes thru final sleep

The dagger twists from friendly hands

From cheerful eyes betrayal lands

What once a friendship, now ignored

The knife, all trust has fully gored

As blood flows red and pools below

Just one answer I have to know

Why as a friend, you stabbed me so

When all along you could just go?

Thoughts and Reflections

My Belle
(Written in High School)

In the city of Montgomery

On a base they call Maxwell

Lives a lady born of gentry

My lovely Southern Belle

A caring heart and loving mind

My Belle, the both she has

With her the two are intertwined

They give her soul Pizazz

A smile from her can cheer you up

Just like a burning fire

Or cocoa in a china cup

Of her warmth, I never tire

Thoughts and Reflections

The Pain in Numbness

Skin on fire with tingling pain

But numbness felt inside the brain

Working slowly as I cry

To distant feet but yet nearby

And hands as far as arms allow

When crippled by pinpricks deep

Dead though living in the now

Awake but yet asleep

Stomach wrenched in agony

And heart ripped into shreds

But yet they function normally

Despite hanging on by threads

My soul is crushed beyond repair

But screams in desperate pain

All the time appearing fair

From loving you again

Thoughts and Reflections

_____

_____

_____

_____

_____

_____

_____

_____

_____

_____

_____

_____

_____

_____

_____

Epiphany

Chugging ahead on the train tracks of life
On wheels that clatter with each little strife
The problems and fears, they pile up in front
Like a home plate scramble when pitched to a bunt

The issues start digging to stop all forward motion
Clawed feet plowing dirt with such fervent devotion
Train going slower as problems surmount
Too many troubles, too much to count

But a light soon dawns in the engineer's mind
Who needs to act quickly as the wheels start to grind
The train of life simply is but one way to ride
And the moon on the trestle show tracks to the side

Reflecting clear tracks, no objects ahead
A perfect clean path with no issues to dread
But how should he get there with no sign of a switch?
His only solution is his train he must ditch

The engineer jumps, and now safely away
He'll walk thru his troubles taking one at a day
He'll find a new train, and keep worries at bay
And follow new tracks that won't lead him astray

The moral I bring you is one simple fact
Jump if you must, but keep on a track
Keep Forward Momentum, and when troubles attack
Just step to the side and give them some slack

The "After" Life

Thoughts and Reflections

_____

_____

_____

_____

_____

_____

_____

_____

_____

_____

_____

_____

_____

_____

STEVEN BATES

Sadness

Fuzzy grayness fills my soul

As darkened thoughts surround me

Depression takes a heavy toll

As heart beats ever slowly

Tears flow free as pain erupts

From within my core so deep

As if my insides rip my guts

And blood from the wound does seep

Clouds grow dark in skies above

As gloom and doom defeat me

For pain so great has come from love

Which left me sad and lonely

For once true love has touched your heart

Then leaves so quick and harshly

The anguish shreds your world apart

And heartbreak tears completely

Thoughts and Reflections

_____

_____

_____

_____

_____

_____

_____

_____

_____

_____

_____

_____

_____

_____

741-741

When life has you hanging
By a fragile thin thread
And you hear creditors banging
As you lay in your bed

The phone won't stop ringing
With late notice calls
At the door, dogs are barking
While echoes bounce down the halls

Stress has your hands wringing
Holding covers over your head
And life has no meaning
But death does instead

With tasks overwhelming
Please pick up your phone
There's a number for texting
Your state of your home
Then send the words to the number
741 741
And wait for the call
That's all needs to be done

Here's hoping the caller
Can help with your pain
And I pray that your future
Is bright once again

Thoughts and Reflections

It is Not Love

It's not love in any special way
If you're holding her hand out in public each day
It's not love if your mouth won't behave
And it's constantly attached to hers like a slave

No, it's not Love if you have to display
If you have to repeat it daily and say it
But what then is love if it's not all of these things?
And what then is love which makes our hearts sing?

True Love is the kind that needs to words or actions
And the littlest things bring immense satisfactions
True Love is the kind that with no words or phrases
Keeps joy in your heart with a smile that amazes

And the tiniest details are loved and adored
Like unconditional Love from our Savior and Lord
Yes, it isn't Love if you have to question its' source
And it isn't Love, but you'd know that of course

If only I could show you what Love isn't to me
I could lift all your doubts about my love to thee
And then you would know that my Love is true,
For what isn't Love, if I don't have it for you?

Thoughts and Reflections

_____

_____

_____

_____

_____

_____

_____

_____

_____

_____

_____

_____

_____

_____

STEVEN BATES

A Little Levity

Breath

You took it first when I saw you
Sitting in that restaurant chair
With the very first "how do you do?"
My lungs gave up their air

You took it next when first we kissed
Just three days after meeting
Again my lungs the air it missed
My heart stopped with its beating

You took it again when "yes" you said
After many a breathless dawn
And even now my breath is bled
When your eyes I look upon

Your body still my breath it takes
When held, my love is greater
My love for you my breath forsakes
Now where is my inhaler?

The "After" Life

Thoughts and Reflections

_____

_____

_____

_____

_____

_____

_____

_____

_____

_____

_____

_____

_____

_____

_____

_____

STEVEN BATES

The Garden

A Giant towering over me
Set me down beside a tree
He turned me once, turned me twice
With zero compassion, for he wasn't too nice

He bellowed a laugh as the more he me turned
Adjusting my face, oh his laughter it burned
He gathered a few of my friends for this show
And placed them in dirt where the bushes don't grow

He lined us all up, a display he was making
I felt for my friends at the Giant's undertaking
He'd turn us, twist us, and shove us hard in the dirt
I have to admit that it really did hurt

Not for the laughter or our feet getting buried
But for the leaving us here that was having me worried
He seemed satisfied with our position and stance
And as he turned fast away I stole a quick glance

To all of my friends, so far from home
But that's the sad life of a poor Garden Gnome
We'll guard all your gardens, your plants, and your tree
And stand ever present for your neighbors to see

So next time you place us, you Giants called Man
Just remember our feelings as we stoically stand

The "After" Life

Thoughts and Reflections

_____

_____

_____

_____

_____

_____

_____

_____

_____

_____

_____

_____

_____

_____

_____

Recitation

I'm supposed to stand upon this stage
And recite my poems as some old sage
To impart my wisdom, my talents true
Passed on like some great gift to you

But those that know me and know me well
Know that I stand here in living Hell
I sweat, I shake, I tremble and stutter
It's hard to hear me as soft I mutter

My speech goes frantic as I rush each verse
Never knowing if my writing you'll praise or curse
My reading skills are my talent indeed
But I read out loud and sweat starts to bead

My voice cracks greatly, it's more scared than I
Reciting my poetries not easy as pie
So here I stand, a nervous ninny
But I thought I'd impart to you the skinny
It's much more difficult to me you see
Than you who sit there hearing me

The "After" Life

Thoughts and Reflections

_____

_____

_____

_____

_____

_____

_____

_____

_____

_____

_____

_____

_____

_____

_____

_____

_____

STEVEN BATES

The Abyss

Behind the jars of mold and rot
Beneath containers of what looks like snot
Between the cartons of curdled creams
Before the stuff of nightmares and dreams

Deep in the corner, stashed and buried
Down in the depths are spices curried
Forgotten finds that bid revealing
Furry mildew that is almost willing

To come to life with vim and vigor
For all it needs is sparks to trigger
A new life form that screams for blood
With all appearance of fuzzy mud

Where is this place of hidden slimes,
That should be marked with dates and times?
With specimens sealed tight with lids
In the great Abyss, we call, the Fridge!

The "After" Life

Thoughts and Reflections

_____

_____

_____

_____

_____

_____

_____

_____

_____

_____

_____

_____

_____

_____

Who Is He?

He grinned like a cat who's found the dairy
Satisfied, gratified and amusingly merry
His smile lit up as the Fourth of July
If you sit back, I'll tell you just why...

Grab you a soda, then stretch out your toes
For here is the guy that everyone knows
He's faithful and friendly, He's the cat's own meows
He's got more charm than any Heaven allows

He's smoother than butter, sweeter than cream
The idol of millions and every girl's dream
He comes in a bottle, but a genie he's not
But muscles galore, and what a smile he's got

An earring to boot with his shiny bald head
But a pirate he's not, that never was said
Starch white crisp clothes adorn his physique
Thus making him shine with radiance unique

He's known much to all and his name you could glean
Cause the dashing old man's name is the famed Mr. Clean!

Thoughts and Reflections

Words

Words once tripped from lips in multitude
But now lay tucked away in solitude
What once spilled out in torrential waves
Now merely sputter as flickering flames

What seemed once a gift of elegant prose
Now is a curse of continuous woes
For writer's block has struck indeed with fervor
Though invisible to the meek observer

It taunts me from the pages blank
With letters floating in darkness dank
It teases with words all incoherent
With meanings jumbled and unapparent

But yet as I sit with hands on temples
A thought emerges with smile dimpled
For while lamenting of this accursed condition
I realized this poem has come to fruition

So I present these words as my cure is revealed
In hopes that your pleasure has now been instilled

The "After" Life

Thoughts and Reflections

STEVEN BATES

Me, My Life, and I

STEVEN BATES

My Past

I left it all, I left my house

Walked right out on my kids and my spouse

I ran with the thought to finish it all

From too much stress, from too far a fall

I thought their lives would be better off

If I wasn't there for them to scoff

I thought my death would bring them life

Instead of dragging down my kids and wife

I looked for ways to do the deed

Like cut my wrists, then lie and bleed

Or jump in front of a moving truck

But no semis drove by, just my luck

Suicide by cop seemed an easy pick

But as I approached his car, he left really quick

He'd never know the guilt my death would have given

But another call had let me stay with the living

I pondered hanging from a tall, tall tree

But the climbing thing I just couldn't see

I wanted another to do the crime

To put me into peace sublime

A coward I was, or so I thought

I just couldn't be the one to make the shot

I broke down again, from the fear of dying

Yet the thoughts of death would ease my crying

I felt that no one understood

Why I'd want to end my life for good

It was logic and plain easy for me to see

But others couldn't and wouldn't let it be

They'd counsel, coerce, console, and cry

When I just felt it was my time to die

Yet somehow amidst all my trouble and strife

I learned to value this thing called life

It took a few visits of in-patient sessions

Of intensive therapy, pills, medications

STEVEN BATES

It took realizing that though I've seen much
My mind and body were just out of touch

I learned that my life is not mine to take
That I need to live for all my loved ones' sake
My parents, my children, my spouse all would hurt
As they lowered me down and threw handfuls of dirt

The flag would be folded and handed down with respect
As my family, my friends would on my life reflect
They'd remember me fondly though with sadness and grief
Shaking their heads in morose disbelief

Yes, my passing would create to them so much pain
By the fact that my dying would bring nothing to gain
Don't get me wrong now, I've thought it all through
And I'm going to live - for me, them, and you.

The "After" Life

Thoughts and Reflections

_____

_____

_____

_____

_____

_____

_____

_____

_____

_____

_____

_____

_____

_____

_____

STEVEN BATES

Death Dream

So softly treads upon my dreams
The nightmares, things of fear and screams
Vanished quick as light hits my eyes
As if forgetting would win a prize

I can't recall the abhorrent frights
Which fill my sleep with chilling sights
I can't explain the sweat-soaked shirts
Which I awaken in, with breath that hurts

I only know the horror I felt
As if on my grave I prayed and knelt
And on the tombstone read an icy fact
For etched on the date, someone had hacked

The date was past, just yesterday
But meant beneath me I did lay
I felt a tremble in the soggy ground
As if in the coffin my corpse did pound

Slamming fists against the wood
Vibrations echoed to where I stood
Then through the dirt a hand did burst
Its icy touch I swore was cursed

It clenched my heel to forbid my run
And I knew my time on Earth was done
Then as sun dawned on my corpse and me
My eyes blinked twice and what did I see?

Around my bed lay wreaths and buds
With dirt in sheets and sleeping duds
A tombstone headboard behind me fell
And I know I screamed a deathly yell

So startled was I by this fearsome scene
I awoke again to sheets all clean
Satin pillow beneath my head
But in my coffin, for I was dead

116

The "After" Life

Thoughts and Reflections

117

Badges

A pointed star once adorned my chest
To defend and serve, I tried my best
Then another badge I wore with pride
'Til a different shield hung upon my hide

I served securing construction sites
Then moved on up to bar room fights
A country club then followed suit
Guarding many a rich and snotty snoot

The Air Reserve then took me in
For another badge on my chest to pin
Performing duties of a combat sort
Instead of enforcing law and tort

Then a City shield, badge 82
Back on the streets to protect you
Trading that in on down the road
When Corrections called from their abode

A county jail, six stories in height
Provided a shield that fit just right
Until that fateful day in late December
Where I joined the Air Force as a Security member

The rest they say is history
That's about all there is to tell of me

Thoughts and Reflections

_____

_____

_____

_____

_____

_____

_____

_____

_____

_____

_____

_____

_____

_____

STEVEN BATES

Evil Within

When diagnosed with diabetes

Immediately begins the treatise

The bargains made with food and drink

Controlling sugars lest you sink

Watching closely for any of these

Infections, threats or even disease

The fading vision, neuropathy

So many risks that threaten me

The heart, the kidney, it's all connected

Amazing how it's all affected

I pray that somehow I'll muddle through

And with firm resolve begin anew

To try living healthier every day

And keep the evil held at bay

The "After" Life

Thoughts and Reflections

Tulia

She was fiercely as loyal as any dog could be
She had a special place of honor in our family
Thirteen years she had lived her life
Pet to both my kids and wife

At peace now, her suffering's gone
For her time in pain would be much too long
A constant companion she'd be thru the night
She'd sleep in-between us, nestled in tight

She'd snort and she'd kick, in sleep she would fight
All manner of threats 'til dawn's morning light
She served as protector and also our friend
A little black pug who was loved to no end

But sadly the day of her long night's sleep came
And with tears in our eyes, we bid farewell to the Dame
The Old Girl of the house, her job now is done
And there's a hole in our heart where her memory's gone

Thoughts and Reflections

STEVEN BATES

Faces

I look upon the faces
Of those that passed away
And I think of all the places
That they've spent their final days

I wonder of their ages
And what brought them here to me
As they faced the final stages
And fade into obscurity

I often think how young they were
How my life and theirs could be
Just the same, in fact I'm sure
We shared some history

And as I ponder and turn the page
Then scan what is to be
The daily news that's all the rage
And affects a lad like me

I reflect again upon the lives
Of those whose destiny
Was to leave their families and their wives
And grace an obituary

Thoughts and Reflections

My Parents

If my parents, this Earth should ever leave
It would break my heart, but I shall not Grieve
For my mom, the angel that she is
Would rise to heaven on wings of bliss

My father, stalwart ever so
Would float to God for him to show
That a worthy couple had walked thru the gate
Full of love and void of hate

A pair that taught their children well
To avoid the slippery slope to Hell
To live with morals and right attitude
Though they may earn the nickname "Prude"

To follow God, to keep His word
To not believe a rumor heard
To use Ma'am and Sir to anyone older
Those that are married, or even a soldier

They taught their young ones to show respect
To never harm a person with abuse, neglect
To always walk next to the Lord
Side by side, thru the unexplored

They lived the path, that rocky road
One with God and that they showed
But they're still alive, thank God for that
Perhaps someday soon I'll tip my hat

To show respect to an amazing pair
And let them know how much I care
They taught us well, they taught us right
They taught us not to fear the Light

So I hope to tell them, and for this I'm glad
They are amazing parents, and I Love them both,
my Mom and Dad

Thoughts and Reflections

_____

_____

_____

_____

_____

_____

_____

_____

_____

_____

_____

_____

_____

_____

_____

_____

_____

The Chief

To some that know him, his title's the Chief
To others, he knows plants, leaf by leaf
To some, he's a deacon and preacher man
To others he's known as a man who CAN

To some, a man that teaches those
Whom while in prison, learn of every rose
Or in colleges where his students learn
The way to nurture both flower and fern

To some, he's known as an enthusiast
Trains, stamps or coin – a Numismatist
His collections vary as does his tastes
To some, he's a veritable knowledge base

He's a master electrician, carpenter too
Able to build a nice home for you
He can wire that house from top to bottom
He knows much more than most have forgotten

A righteous man, forgiving in nature
Learned in multiple nomenclature
Of science, history, Biblical fact
Archeological finds and rare artifact

He's known by all as a man of his word
His lines of morality are not to be blurred
Respectful of others, his manners ensure
That respect is due him, for most call him Sir

His scruples intact, his name not besmirched
From friends or foes, pious or unchurched
His titles were earned by the careers that he had
But my favorite he earned, was that I call him Dad

Thoughts and Reflections

_____

_____

_____

_____

_____

_____

_____

_____

_____

_____

_____

_____

_____

_____

_____